The Eternal Madness

Vandana Kalsi

Ukiyoto Publishing

All global publishing rights are held by

Ukiyoto Publishing

Published in 2023

Content Copyright © Vandana

ISBN: 9789360498191

All rights reserved.
No part of this publication may be reproduced, transmitted, or stored in a retrieval system, in any form by any means, electronic, mechanical, photocopying, recording or otherwise, without the prior permission of the publisher.

The moral rights of the author have been asserted.

This is a work of fiction. Names, characters, businesses, places, events, locales, and incidents are either the products of the author's imagination or used in a fictitious manner. Any resemblance to actual persons, living or dead, or actual events is purely coincidental.

This book is sold subject to the condition that it shall not by way of trade or otherwise, be lent, resold, hired out or otherwise circulated, without the publisher's prior consent, in any form of binding or cover other than that in which it is published.

www.ukiyoto.com

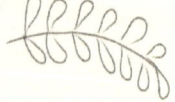

To every soul that wriggles in pain,
It's all temporary, trust me, it will fade.
Whenever you feel that it's all in vain,
Just remember, Never be afraid.
Face the pain that binds you in chains
And you will never be the same.

Acknowledgement

I'd like to thank my friends for their support and encouragement. My publishing house whose constructive feedback greatly improved the manuscript. A special thanks to the open source images that inspired many of the illustrations.

Finally, I extend my heartfelt gratitude to the readers, whose interest in this book drives my passion for writing. Thank you for embarking on this journey with me.

Contents

The Whispers of Broken Bonds	1
Love, Lust and Loss	27
Deep Dark and Dangerous	43
The Winds Of Possibilities	70
About the Author	*84*

vandana

The Whispers of Broken Bonds

2
The Eternal Madness

Every night, I sit on the corner of my bed,

Looking at the moon, shine bright red.

With the blood that I once held so dear,

Turned to a nightmare that I feared.

I look at my scars, remembering despair,

Waiting for a time to heal my tears.

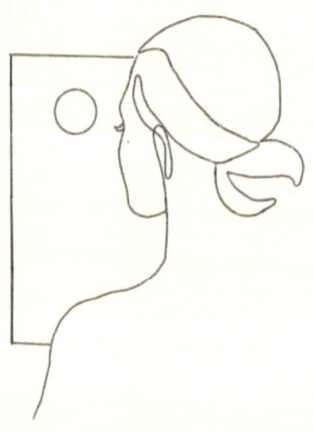

vandana

All my life, I've live with lies,
Believing that love never dies,
Hoped for her affection, a lifelong time.
Her eyes now hold disdain's cruel disguise,
As if my presence tarnished skies,
Her blue gaze reminds me of a time,
When her love was only mine.

The Eternal Madness

Throughout my life, your judgement fell,
A shade darker, they'd often tell,
Sharper edges, I dared to show,
Yet you questioned the seeds I'd sow,
Working smarter, I aimed to be,
Loving you fiercely, endlessly,
Yet you hated, my very existence,
leaving me alone, far distant.

vandana

The darkness spreads, within the flesh that remains,
Sucking out all life, with no love to suffice.
The pain grows, as my cherished one forgoes,
Leaving me in the coldness of a lifeless snow.
I can hear the crows gnaw,
Plunging the rose, that once I held so close.
Beneath this coldness, my sorrow flows,
Into a red river that will never be known.

The Eternal Madness

The innocent eyes that once I adored,
Now look at me with hateful remorse,
With disgust, a thousand fold.
She tore me apart, with her gentle force,
The love that once build my home,
Lays shattered, in a delusion of hope.

vandana

In the depths of my being, her warmth resides,
A feeling I cherished once, to always guide.
Yet her expression eludes my mind,
Like a whispered breeze that was once kind.

The Eternal Madness

I miss our small talks
I miss the late night long walks
I miss your cosy embrace
And the fact, you can never be replaced

vandana

I yearned for our eyes to meet,

Yet fate's message is bitter and sweet.

Wandered, seeking a sight so divine,

Marbles of innocence, radiant like the skies.

In a fleeting fraction, my heart certainly knows,

That a love that flickers briefly, will always leave me alone.

I wish, I could go back in time,
Rewind every moment, make you mine.

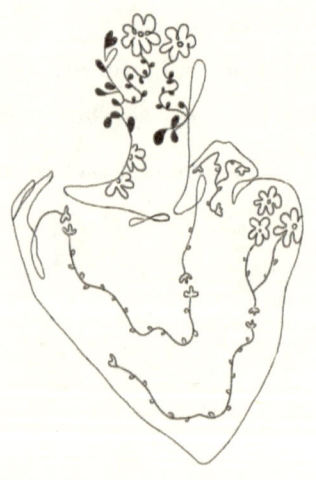

vandana

My sorrow isn't born from your despair,
But knowing that the love I yearn for is rare.

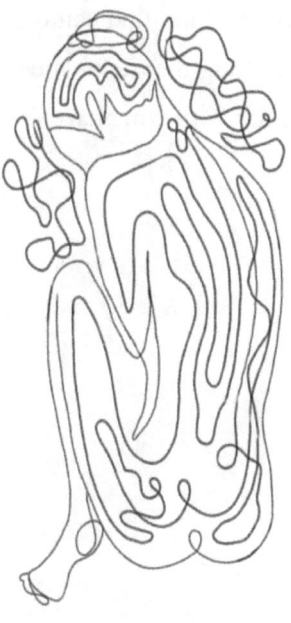

The Eternal Madness

I have read thousands of books
Seen hundreds with good looks
Wandered all alone in the woods
Yet nothing that can calm my heart,
Nothing that helps me start,
A life with you apart.

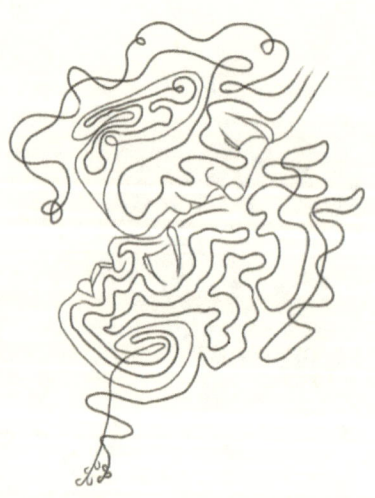

vandana

Once, her embrace was the warmth of divine,
Now she detests the life I'd designed,
Yet I hold on to the belief she cared,
Even if brief, it was a love we once shared.

14
The Eternal Madness

Maybe, I just don't deserve anything.

vandana

Beneath this moonlit, enchanting light,
Your innocent eyes, a captivating sight.
Wishing, just for tonight, it's all real and near,
A beautiful memory in my heart, forever dear.

16
The Eternal Madness

Do you desire to glimpse my dreams,
Or merely listen to my silent screams?
Perhaps you aim to paint a different scene,
Where it's always me who takes the leave.

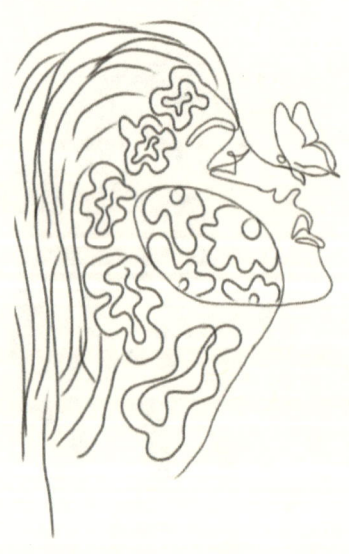

vandana

In the smallest joys, I glimpse you anew,
In failures and doubt, I yearn for you too.
In my deepest regrets, your absence I rue,
Even when you're not here, I'll forever sense you.

The Eternal Madness

I longed for you, yet my body bore disdain,

Perhaps it's time to part from your hurtful reign,

For the pain in my heart surpasses the bruises you've laid,

And now, I listen to the whispers of these bruised scars, unafraid,

Reminding myself of the love that you never displayed.

vandana

All my life, you claimed I wasn't enough,
Perhaps my love for you felt somewhat rough.
 Still, I gave my heart and soul to your control,
Yet you crushed my being beneath your sole.

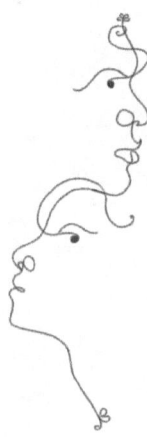

The Eternal Madness

It's been years since I last spoke to you,
Perhaps I still stir up those fluttering blues,
Maybe, I make your heart skip a beat,
Or perhaps it's just a mirage, incomplete.

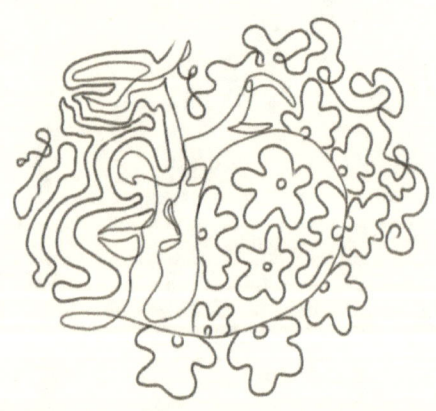

vandana

The space between us now vast and wide,
Strangers we've become, side by side.

The Eternal Madness

I'll never forget how you gazed at her,
Though she never loved you, your feelings did stir.
Your sympathy worsened this unrequited love's curse,
Shattering me into pieces, I'll never be able to nurse.

vandana

I desired you so deeply, it drove me insane,
Your love and care left me in a mesmerising chain.
Our bodies entwine in a beautiful tangled mess,
Your tender touch led to my every success.
You were the one I yearned for, night and day,
Years have passed, yet your presence won't fade away,
In the flickering lights, you continue to stay.

The Eternal Madness

Do you grasp the sorrow in this futile life,

Even when I erased every trace of your deceit and strife.

With all my might, I forgave your past mistakes,

Yet you'll never comprehend the silence my nights still make.

vandana

You despised my very existence in your world,
Yet I never grasped the hatred you unfurled.

The Eternal Madness

You remind me of my helplessness,
The deep fissures in my hollow emptiness,
It is a vacuum of despair, that refuses to transpire
Echoing the memories of my defeat that never expire

Love, Lust and Loss

The Eternal Madness

A love so gentle, forever true,
A certainty, it's always you,
In your presence, my pain finds its cure,
May this connection forever remain pure.

vandana

Tell me you will love me always,
And never let any of this fade away.

The Eternal Madness

Submerge me in your love, like gin in a glass so deep,

Draw me near in your warm embrace, like the secrets you keep.

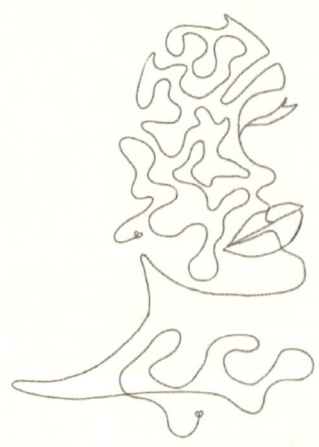

vandana

Sometimes I wonder, will I find a warm embrace?
That sweeps me off the ground and makes my heart race.

The Eternal Madness

I want someone whom I can openly trust,

And when I'm angry, they embrace me with warm hugs,

A person with whom pretence does not exist,

Their gentle touch makes the world cease to persist.

vandana

Your smile makes me go crazy,
And my heart flutters like a baby,
For once, I knew he felt the same,
And loved me like, I was his to claim,
Even Though your feelings seem to change,
The only truth I know is that you make me insane.

The Eternal Madness

If I'm quick, I survive this endless torture
If not this is my end, in the echoes of her laughter.

vandana

As a child, life was blissfully simple,
Cotton candy, hugs, a carefree wimple.
Now, entwined in the web of darkness,
I seek that lost innocence, endless.

The Eternal Madness

Once, it was love so pure and true,
Now, I cringe at the very sight of you.

vandana

All my life, I've heard the call for faith,
To trust in myself, never to hesitate,
To forge myself with strength and grace,
To rise on tiptoes, embracing every ache.
Yet the weight of my failure, binds me in a chain,
Transforms me into a creature, driving me insane.

The Eternal Madness

Have you ever travelled back in your thoughts,
Rewinding moments, making memories last,
Where happiness in life was dearly bought,
And contentment found its forever cast.

vandana

Wherever you are in this universe,
There will always be a part of me,
That will wait for you under this beautiful sky,
Where our eternal memories, shine high,
Just like a beautiful bliss, that never dies.

The Eternal Madness

You are beautiful just as you are,

Never change for those who consider you a farce,

Your imperfections are beautiful, they set you apart,

Like a beautiful diamond that shines bright in the dark.

vandana

Walls painted with memories of our dreams,
Amid the cold mist and clouds that seem,
Like colourful stars in constellations above,
Evoking memories of a time we once loved.

The Eternal Madness

I want you to touch me, longer,
I want you to love me, harder,
Maybe for a moment, pretend it's not torture.

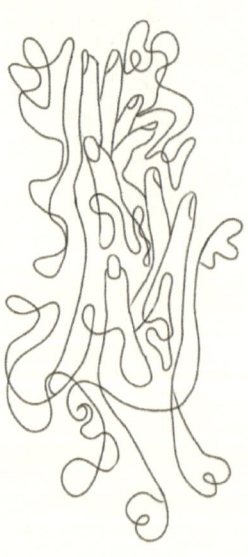

vandana

Deep Dark and Dangerous

The Eternal Madness

Sometimes, I wish for death,
To take away my breath,
carry me far from the rest.
To a place where no one knows me,
A place where someone loves me,
A place where nothing matters anymore.
And I am free just like a floating cloud,
Flying in the depths of the sky,
Away from this writhing lie.

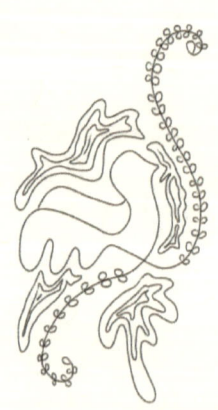

vandana

On every step, of my recoil,
On every pain of my exploit,
On every defeat of my joy.
It is a soft tiny voice,
That forcing me to die,
To vanish from this lie,
And never be alive.

The Eternal Madness

What if I falter, betray, or evade,
From responsibilities, I once obeyed,
It is a grand scheme of illusion it seems,
A dream I'm chasing with lifeless themes,
Through mistakes I toil for effort and endeavour,
To refine this dream and make it better, forever.

vandana

I see the fame, I see the lust,
I see the pain, I see the mistrust,
All of it in a tiny world of dust.
Moving towards a delusion of hope,
Where you and I will always mope.
For things that we hold so close,
Alas, Nothing will matter anymore,
Once we're gone from this darkened hole.

The Eternal Madness

All my life, I have been a coward,
Wishing for death to come and devour,
Never grateful, for the things I own,
Complaining, till the end of dawn.
Pushing away the ones I love,
Never realised, the world above,
Waiting for the time to pass,
Only to realise the loved ones never last.

vandana

Do you see the scars on my soul,
They tell a story that's not so old.
My heart remains sore,
Looking for love, that will never be my own.
My screams echo the pains of my past,
A painful feeling that will always last.

The Eternal Madness

Whenever, I look in the mirror,
I see a girl that's not so clear.
Her innocent eyes, filled with tears,
Her beautiful curls, entangled in fear,
Her radiant smile, that seems unreal,
Her anxious thought, entwined in despair.
Can you see her, sinking to endear,
For the ones that no longer care.
Look close, do you see her clear,
She awaits for time to disappear,
And wishes for life that's more real.

vandana

I wish this was simple,
To evaporate my existence
Crawl into a tiny black hole
Where no one cares anymore
Somewhere I can live free,
Away from any scrutiny,
Away from your expectancy,
Away from a tiring journey.
A place where no one knows me.

The Eternal Madness

I sense my life at an abrupt standstill,
I'm losing all control, now it's just a bitter pill.
On a treadmill of monotony, I tread,
An unnerving ache urging to be shed.
My cherished dreams, dormant and chilled,
Life is stale, no excitement to be fulfilled.

vandana

At day's end, it matters not if guilt, anxiety, or sorrow abound.

People disregard your struggles and success, as they're bound.

Perhaps glad for your woes, to sprint in this race of disdain,

Leaving the emotionally burdened, behind in their pain.

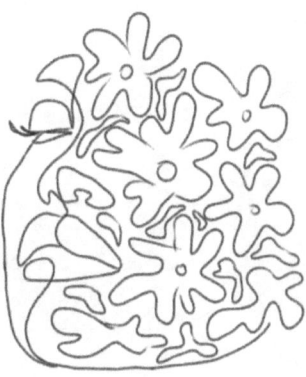

The Eternal Madness

Have you felt pain that twists and turns,
Leaving your mind in knots that burn?
Towards a hope of light, you take a stride,
But it pulls you deeper, far and wide.
A life of happiness, slowly fades,
Love's tender touch, a distant shade.

vandana

Anxiety and doubt bore a hole within,
Sucking me into a vacuum where sadness begins.

The Eternal Madness

In her beauty and purity, she's adorned,
While I feel unattractive and scorned,
To be her is a distant dream,
A life I'll never fully esteem,
I can't be her, that much is true,
Her life's a dream I can't pursue.
Desire lingers, a persistent flame,
Wishing to relive that lust for fame.

vandana

The epitome of elegance resides,
In her, beauty and radiance collides,
Kindness and love, a gentle stream,
Her soft chuckle, like a peaceful dream.
As I draw near, her visage blurs,
Unravelling demons that silently stir,
Shrouding all joy, casting a fearful shade,
Pushing me back, making me evade.
Hoping to see her beautiful face,
A facade crumbles, not staying the same,
A revelation that caught me off guard,
Behind the veneer, a reality scarred.

The Eternal Madness

Do you see the waves of hope,
Crushing my faith, like the sea on shore.
Every step I take to forget the pain,
Brings me back, all over again.
Anxiously, I make my way,
To a place that seems so far away.

vandana

I wish for ease when, I crumble and fall,
To release my cries and let tears flow all.
Let me rise from the depths and crawl with might,
Embrace myself in the darkest of nights,
Believe in hope like a beacon so clear,
Guide me a way through doubt and fear.

The Eternal Madness

I stumble and shatter,
Compensating tears in a silent patter,
My Heart grips, a relentless strain,
Chained to thoughts that cause me pain,
In a shadow of bitterness, I once dwelled,
A place I hope to leave, no longer closely held,
I rise breaking from the weight,
Into an enduring shadow, where strength awaits.

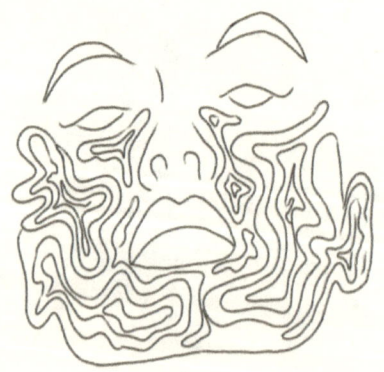

This storm's embrace, a gleaming sight,
Moonlight pierces through, casting its light,
Unveiling the past, as the shadow cast,
An eternal saga that will forever last.

The Eternal Madness

I've grown with verses that paint the grandeur,
The mystique, selflessness of skies so pure,
Yet today, I glimpse little more,
Lust and fear surround the cosmic lore.

vandana

Just like the wind's gentle sigh,

A memory of you makes me cry.

Unwilling to accept, unwilling to believe,

That you might depart, that I might grieve.

I look at the moon's tender gleam,

That will Illuminate my hope, sadly, a recurring dream.

The Eternal Madness

Do you dream of happiness,
A place so serene, filled with kindness.
A realm where I can sense a human embrace,
Conversations free-flowing, with unhurried pace.
Through my veins, love's pulse shall wend,
Slowly, overpowering every nerve's end.
A state of abyss, is what I crave,
Wishing for beautiful bliss, to always stay.

vandana

The zenith of this pain is enormous,
And the struggle remains endless.
I have Spiralled through an eternity,
Running away from my absurdity,
To a space of lustful insanity,
somewhere far from reality.
Wishing to break away from this fantasy
And see beyond the agony and misery
Realising you will always remain here, with me.

The Eternal Madness

Can you see my defected soul?
It craves a love, that's not my own.
An Aching heart that is forever sore,
Seeking love, a dream never explored.
Sadly, these screams bear the past of distress,
A lingering ache, a timeless duress.

vandana

Every day, I hope the pain disappears,
Evaporates in the sky, and never appear,
My success will never suffice my greed,
While my failures make me bleed.
The happiness, I felt now seems oblivious,
Sadly, the pain makes this beautiful place hideous.

The Eternal Madness

I wish to end this pain, that's driving me insane,
Sadly, I no longer have the courage, to end this enrage
And to lift up a knife, and end this worthless life.

vandana

Sometimes I wish you held me close,
Calmed me and whispered that I'm not alone.

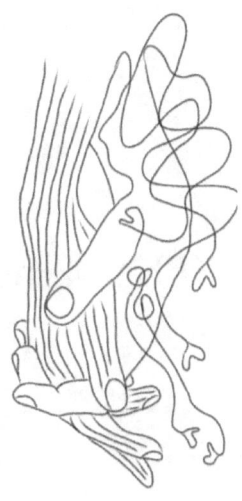

The Winds Of Possibilities

vandana

Just as the moon's phases tell a tale,
In this journey I will stumble and fail,
But with time's tender touch, I hope to sail,
Rising from ashes, stronger than the gale.

The Eternal Madness

Raindrops pierce my veins, a gentle touch,
Drowning me in thoughts so rough.
The thoughts sink within, drowning me in vain,
Thoughts of pain entwine my tumultuous brain.
Regrets of yesterday, a wandering flame,
Never to be the same, they whisper in claim.
Yet, in this downpour, I yearn to attain,
A cleansing release from this mental chain.
Hoping the rain carry the burden, the disdain,
To a realm where sanity will forever reign.

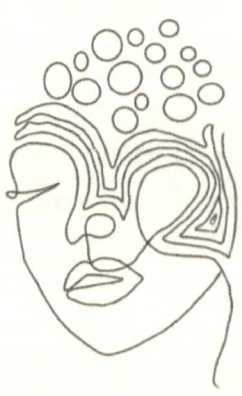

vandana

In a world that's extraordinary and vast,
I'm just a fleeting soul, not meant to last.
Yet deep within, a spark ignites,
A yearning for new scale and heights.
Pondering of endless possibilities, I see,
Hoping for a future that's lasting, where I'm meant to be.

The Eternal Madness

Weary of this world, so it seems,
Longing for a dreamworld, of boundless dreams.
Where I can soar through the azure sky,
Far away, where constraints can't pry.
A realm distant from life's demands,
Vanished, beyond where anyone stands.

vandana

I gaze upon my reflection, a void of distress,
Doubt, fear, anger, and lust in chaotic excess.

The Eternal Madness

Wealth, love, desire, and greed, all in time, turn to dust,

But the kindness shared lingers in memories, like an everlasting trust.

vandana

When my problems bring sadness and anxiety,
I picture those facing far greater adversity,
They retain their grace, and never lose their pace,
Fighting through challenges until they find their place.

The Eternal Madness

Within the vast universe, it's a endless fight,
For survival and to persevere with all their might.
Embracing all pain, in an eternal mud,
To emerge transformed, a beautiful bud.

vandana

I need to live my moments and forget about the past.
Before I realised, everything just swept away as fast.
And now I regret all that lost time, that once last.

The Eternal Madness

A timeless act of kindness, forever alive,
Cherished memories, in our hearts they thrive,
A need we all share, a touch of fondness,
But what we truly seek is genuine happiness.

vandana

Let this world turn to dust,
And it's just you and me, untouched,
As we listen to the echoes of our heartbeat
Reminiscing every moment you had with me.

The Eternal Madness

In your first breath, my heart found love,
Tiny hands I wish, never grow rough
A forever love that will never decay,
You're a part of me even when you're away.
You're my lovely miracle, my lifelong dream,
You are my happiness, my tiny ray of beam.

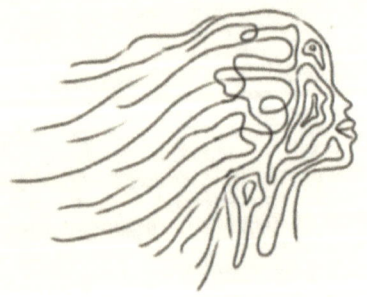

vandana

May the universe take you,
To the happiness you never knew.

About the Author

Vandana, is an aspiring author who recently embarked on her literary journey. With a passion for poetry, she is dedicated to honing her craft and bringing her imaginative worlds to life on paper. She is a graduate from Delhi and writes during her free time. Her love for books and creativity has been her driving force, and she is excited to share her poems with readers as she continues to explore the art of writing.

www.ingramcontent.com/pod-product-compliance
Lightning Source LLC
LaVergne TN
LVHW041625070526
838199LV00052B/3242